KT-231-374

A SECOND SCOTTISH POETRY BOOK

compiled by

Alan Bold

Oxford University Press   1985

Oxford University Press, Walton Street, Oxford OX2 6DP

Oxford   New York   Toronto
Delhi   Bombay   Calcutta   Madras   Karachi
Nairobi   Dar es Salaam   Cape Town
Kuala Lumpur   Singapore   Hong Kong   Tokyo
Melbourne   Auckland

and associates in
Beirut   Berlin   Ibadan   Mexico City   Nicosia

© Oxford University Press 1985

Phototypeset by Tradespools Ltd, Frome, Somerset
Printed in Hong Kong

British Library Cataloguing in Publication Data
A Second Scottish poetry book.
1. Scottish poetry   2. English poetry –
Scottish authors
I. Bold, Alan
821'.00809411   PR8650

A Second Scottish Poetry Book
ISBN 0-19-917070-3 (net)
ISBN 0-19-917069-X (non-net)

The publishers would like to thank Glasgow Museums and Art
Galleries for permission to reproduce *Hesperus, the Evening Star,
Sacred to Lovers* by Sir Joseph Noel Paton on p. 93, and the National
Galleries of Scotland, Edinburgh for permission to reproduce a detail of
Sailing Ships and Mermaids by Robert Burns on p. 43, and *Wandering
Shadows* by Peter Graham on p. 121.

The publishers would also like to thank the following for permission
to reproduce photographs:

Aerofilms, p. 22–23; K.M. Andrew, pp. 28, 77; F.E. Bayley, p. 86;
British Tourist Authority, p. 41; Bruce Coleman Ltd., p. 65; Aase
Goldsmith, p. 107; Alistair Gray, pp. 54–55, 94; Keystone Press
Agency, pp. 19, 70–71, 82; Lea MacNally, p. 63; Jessie Ann Matthews,
pp. 86, 111; Gunnie Moberg, p. 45.

For text acknowledgements see pp. 128.

Contents

To the Generation Knocking at
  the Door   *John Davidson*   6
Hope and Patience   *George MacDonald*   7
Scotland small?   *Hugh MacDiarmid*   8
My Native Land   *Sir Walter Scott*   9
Scottish National Anthem   *Alan Bold   Francis George*
     Scott   10

Freedom   *John Barbour*   12
Hame, Hame, Hame   *Allan Cunningham*   13
You're Late Again Kathleen   *John Bett*   14
TV   *Iain Crichton Smith*   15
Television People   *Tessa Ransford*   16
Top of the Pops   *Alexander Scott*   17
Ulaidh/Treasure   *Ruaraidh MacThomais*
     Derick Thomson   18

Proverb   *Walter Perrie*   19
A Summary of *A Midsummer*
  Night's Dream   *Iain Crichton Smith*   21
gleann fadamach/glen remote   *Aonghas MacNeacail*   22
Glider   *Alan Bold*   23
'I could tell'   *R.D. Laing*   24
Lost Gloves   *Douglas Dunn*   25
The philosopher stops work to look
  out of the window   *Kathleen Jamie*   26
Winter-Time   *Marion Angus*   29
The Educators   *David Black*   31
At School   *Iain Crichton Smith*   33
This Nor That   *Alan Jackson*   34
Spaceman   *J.K. Annand*   35
At tea-time   *Alastair Mackie*   36
Little by Little   *Ken Morrice*   38
When I leave school   *Iain Crichton Smith*   39
Small Boy and Lighthouse   *Sydney Tremayne*   40
Sea Ballad   *A.D. Mackie*   42
Wave/Rock   *Ian Hamilton Finlay*   44
Hungry Waters   *Hugh MacDiarmid*   45
The Years of the Crocodile   *Sydney Goodsir Smith*   46
Whales   *Norman MacCaig*   48
Submarine   *Tom Buchan*   49

The Clown	*Maurice Lindsay*	50
The Loch Ness Monster	*Tom Buchan*	52
The Boat's Blueprint	*Ian Hamilton Finlay*	53
The Talk of the Headlands	*George Campbell Hay*	54
Seaweed	*William Jeffrey*	55
waterwheels in whirl	*Ian Hamilton Finlay*	56
Cart Wheels	*William Neill*	57
The Wooden Curlew	*Robin Bell*	58
'great'	*Alan Jackson*	60
The Eagle, Crow, and Shepherd	*Michael Bruce*	61
The Bubblyjock	*Hugh MacDiarmid*	62
The Eagle	*William Sharp*	63
The Owl	*Robin Bell*	65
UFO	*William Montgomerie*	66
Great Frog Race	*Ian Hamilton Finlay*	68
Pigsny-pogsny	*Alastair Fowler*	69
Blind Horse	*Norman MacCaig*	71
The Horses	*Edwin Muir*	72
The Raiders	*Will H. Ogilvie*	74
Hal o' the Wynd	*William Soutar*	75
Hopes	*Tom Scott*	76
Brigs o'Braid	*Forbes Macgregor*	78
End of a cold night	*Norman MacCaig*	80
The Guy	*George MacBeth*	81
War-Dream	*Andrew Greig*	83
Precisely To Scale	*John Whitworth*	84
Think On Me	*Lady John Scott*	86
The Two Brothers	*Anon.*	88
Crowdieknowc	*Hugh MacDiarmid*	90
The Flowers of the Forest	*Jane Elliot*	91
Lochinvar	*Sir Walter Scott*	92
When I Roved a Young Highlander	*George Gordon, Lord Byron*	94
Tribute	*Alan Jackson*	96
The Good Thief	*Tom Leonard*	97
The Great Ones	*John Buchan*	98
The Massacre of the Macpherson	*W.E. Aytoun*	99
Sunny Day	*Duncan Glen*	101

Gethsemane	*J.F. Hendry*	102
Anns A' Phàirce Mhóir/In the Big Park	*Somhairle MacGhill-Eain Sorley MacLean*	103
Kirk Bell	*George Mackay Brown*	104
Wadir-Wise	*William J. Tait*	105
November	*Walter Perrie*	105
Why the Poet Makes Poems	*George Bruce*	106
Silva	*Alastair Fowler*	107
Disbuddin	*Duncan Glen*	107
After the Market	*William Neill*	108
All the Families	*David Craig*	109
Snapshot	*Ken Morrice*	110
Late Autumn	*J.F. Hendry*	110
Savings	*Douglas Dunn*	111
The Green Gate	*George Mackay Brown*	112
Epistle to a Young Friend	*Robert Burns*	114
A Country Tale	*George Mackay Brown*	117
'The vales, the vocal hills'	*Michael Bruce*	121
Archives	*Edwin Morgan*	122

Glossary of Scots Words   123
Index of First Lines   125
Acknowledgements   128

To the Generation Knocking at the Door

Break – break it open; let the knocker rust:
Consider no 'shalt not', and no man's 'must':
And, being entered, promptly take the lead,
Setting aside tradition, custom, creed;
Nor watch the balance of the huckster's beam;
Declare your hardiest thought, your proudest dream:
Await no summons; laugh at all rebuff;
High hearts and youth are destiny enough.
The mystery and the power enshrined in you
Are old as time and as the moment new:
And none but you can tell what part you play,
Nor can you tell until you make assay,
For this alone, this always, will succeed,
The miracle and magic of the deed.

John Davidson

Hope and Patience

An unborn bird lies crumpled and curled,
A-dreaming of the world.

Round it, for castle-wall, a shell
Is guarding it well.

Hope is the bird with its dim sensations;
The shell that keeps it alive is *Patience*.

George MacDonald

Scotland small?
[from *Dìreadh*]

Scotland small? Our multiform, our infinite Scotland *small*?
Only as a patch of hillside may be a cliché corner
To a fool who cries 'Nothing but heather!' where in September another
Sitting there and resting and gazing round
Sees not only the heather but blaeberries
With bright green leaves and leaves already turned scarlet
Hiding ripe blue berries; and amongst the sage-green leaves
Of the bog-myrtle the golden flowers of the tormentil shining;
And on the small bare places, where the little Blackface sheep
Found grazing, milkworts blue as summer skies;
And down in neglected peat-hags, not worked
Within living memory, sphagnum moss in pastel shades
Of yellow, green, and pink; sundew and butterwort
Waiting with wide-open sticky leaves for their tiny winged prey;
And nodding harebells vying in their colour
With the blue butterflies that poise themselves delicately upon them;
And stunted rowans with harsh dry leaves of glorious colour.
'Nothing but heather!' – How marvellously descriptive! And incomplete!

Hugh MacDiarmid

My Native Land
[from *The Lay of the Last Minstrel*]

Breathes there the man, with soul so dead,
Who never to himself hath said,
'This is my own, my native land!'
Whose heart hath ne'er within him burned,
As home his footsteps he hath turned,
    From wandering on a foreign strand! —
If such there breathe, go, mark him well;
For him no minstrel raptures swell;
High though his titles, proud his name,
Boundless his wealth as wish can claim;
Despite those titles, power, and pelf,
The wretch, concentred all in self,
Living, shall forfeit fair renown,
And, doubly dying, shall go down
To the vile dust, from whence he sprung,
Unwept, unhonoured, and unsung.

O Caledonia! stern and wild,
Meet nurse for a poetic child!
Land of brown heath and shaggy wood,
Land of the mountain and the flood,
Land of my sires! what mortal hand
Can e'er untie the filial band,
That knits me to thy rugged strand!

Sir Walter Scott

Scottish National Anthem

Land of great heathered hills,
Land of deep weathered glens,
Old battles still fought on the moors;
See the spirit of the country
Reach out from the past
To the future we feel in us now.

Scotland, Scotland: come to life again.
Scotland, Scotland: gather as a clan.
See the spirit of the country
Reach out from the past
To the future we feel in us now.

As the cities awake,
As the towns come alive,
The lion is rampant once more;
Men and women, sons and daughters,
Recover a cause
And discover its meaning at last.

Now the future is here
And the land come to life
The people sing out with one voice;
Now the country is a nation
Alive to itself
And the chorus sweeps forward in time.

words: Alan Bold

Or in A♭

Solo Voice

Chorus

music: Francis George Scott

10/6/48

Freedom
[from *The Bruce*]

A! fredome is a noble thing!
Fredome maiss man to haif liking:
Fredome all solace to man giffis:
He levis at ease that freely levis!
A noble heart may haif nane ease,
Na ellis nocht that may him please,
Gif fredome failye; for free liking
Is yearnit owre all other thing.
Na he, that ay has levit free,
May nocht knaw weil the propertie,
The anger, na the wrechit dome,
That is couplit to foul thyrldome.
Bot gif he had assayit it,
Than all perquer he suld it wit;
And suld think fredome mar to prize
Than all the gold in warld that is.
Thus contrar thingis ever-mar
Discoveringis of the tother are.

John Barbour

Hame, Hame, Hame

Hame, hame, hame, hame fain wad I be,
O hame, hame, hame, to my ain countrie!

When the flower is i' the bud and the leaf is on the tree,
The larks shall sing me hame in my ain countrie;
Hame, hame, hame, hame fain wad I be,
O hame, hame, hame, to my ain countrie!

The green leaf o' loyaltie's begun for to fa',
The bonnie white rose it is withering an' a';
But I'll water 't wi' the blude of usurping tyrannie,
An' green it will grow in my ain countrie.

O there's naught now frae ruin my country can save,
But the keys o' kind heaven to open the grave,
That a' the noble martyrs who died for loyaltie
May rise again and fight for their ain countrie.

The great now are gane – a' wha ventured to save;
The new grass is springing on the tap o' their grave;
But the sun thro' the mirk blinks blythe in my e'e:
'I'll shine on ye yet in your ain countrie.'

Allan Cunningham

You're Late Again Kathleen

And she came home
the April on her face
and the jam stain
on the side of her mouth
like blood
saying
she'd had tea
at some-one's mother's house
and she had no idea
had she
of what time it was.

And we stood there
stupid in our fury
clutching our time machines
as if we had an idea
of what time was.

John Bett

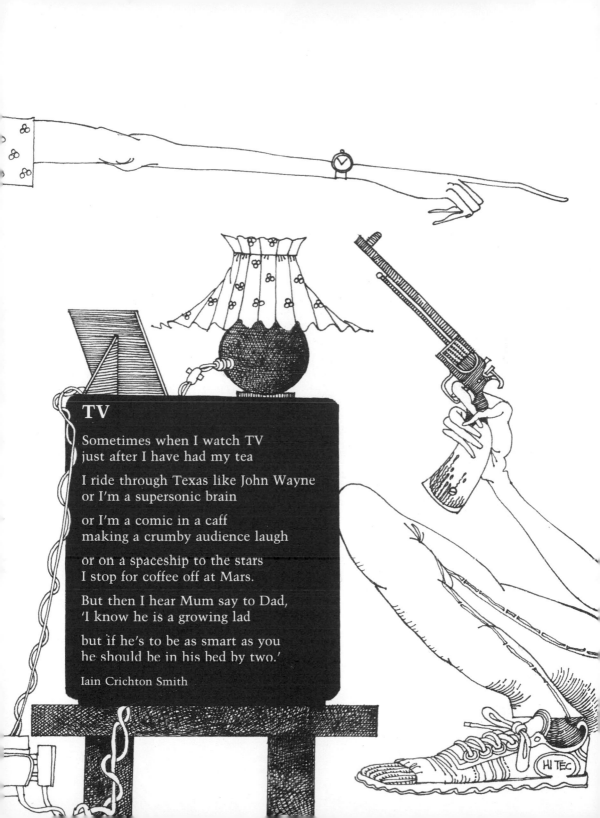

TV

Sometimes when I watch TV
just after I have had my tea

I ride through Texas like John Wayne
or I'm a supersonic brain

or I'm a comic in a caff
making a crumby audience laugh

or on a spaceship to the stars
I stop for coffee off at Mars.

But then I hear Mum say to Dad,
'I know he is a growing lad

but if he's to be as smart as you
he should be in his bed by two.'

Iain Crichton Smith

Television People

We who live by the eye
shall perish from blindness.

Our hands hang useless as we stare
at reality out of reach.

We walk through studio country
dying from lack of dimension.

We hear no voices
that have not been recorded.

We feel no texture
but cold glass of the screen.

We cannot meet each other
for we look in the same direction.

We sit and sit
until final close-down
unless someone
stronger than us
rises
to switch the whole world off.

Tessa Ransford

Top of the Pops

Lowpers, gowpers,
Duntily dowpers.

Skirlers, dirlers,
Bumpily birlers.

Yowlers, growlers,
Sappily sowlers.

Ravers, clavers,
Hotchily havers.

Jiggers, figures,
Trippily triggers.

Beggars, fleggers,
Langily leggers.

Yarkers, warkers,
Stoundily starkers.

Maeners, grainers,
Lowdenly laners.

Daters, maters,
Neibourly naiturs.

Craiturs, craiturs.

Alexander Scott

17

Ulaidh

Bha 'n ulaidh an leth-fhalach
mar gach nì luachmhor,
theann thu suas rith',
rud beag diùid, nàir
aig oisinn na stràid,
a' cuimhneachadh ort fhèin
là, bliadhna a bh'ann,
saoghal a chaill thu;
sheall mi 'n taobh eile;
cha mhòr nach do ghabh thu seachad,
ach bha d' fheum làidir,
's le sùil bheag an taobh a bhà mi
chuir thu do làmh ann
's thug thu bloigh arain as an sprùilleach
is chagainn thu d'uaill fo na mùgan.

Ruaraidh MacThomais

Treasure

The treasure was half-hidden
like all precious things,
you sidled up to it,
a little uncertain, ashamed
at the street corner,
remembering yourself
on another day, another year,
in a world you lost;
I looked the other way;
you almost walked past,
but your need was great,
and throwing a glance in my direction
you put your hand in
and took a piece of bread from among the rubbish
and chewed your pride under lowering eyebrows.

Derick Thomson

Proverb

We are all in the stars
but some of us are
looking at the gutter.

Walter Perrie

A **Summary of** *A Midsummer Night's Dream*

Some stuff about the moon
with fairies and a queen,

and thickheads with queer names.
A Duke on about dreams.

A nut with an Ass's head.
'I tell you,' Willie said,

'them Greeks is a funny lot.
They all get lost, an' that.'

Iain Crichton Smith

gleann fadamach

pléin a dol tarsuing
cho àrd 's nach cluinnear i
long a dol sìos an cuan
ach fada mach air fàire

cuid dhe'n t-saoghal
a suibhal 's a siubhal

's a bhaile so
chan eileas a siubhal ach an aon uair
's na clachan a rinn ballaichean
a dol 'nan càirn

Aonghas MacNeacail

glen remote

plane crossing
so high it can't be heard
ship going down the ocean
far out on the horizon

a part of the world
travelling travelling

in this village
people only travel once
and the stones that made walls
become cairns

Aonghas MacNeacail

Glider

There's a hill in the Lomonds
  Where a glider hangs round;
It plays, as it flies,
  A glissando of sound.

There's a theme as the wind
  Lifts up the front wings;
There's a note that the soloist
  Soulfully sings.

The melody's hushed,
  Sotto voce and slow;
A chorus of birds
  Flutters below.

The clouds, like an audience,
  Are everywhere
As the mind of the pilot
  Orchestrates air.

Alan Bold

23

'I could tell'

I could tell
           from your eyes
you fell
           from the skies

   out of the blue
   there were you

but I knew it wasn't true
and away
       you flew

R.D. Laing

Lost Gloves

I leave my body in a new blue suit
   With my soul, which is newly destitute.
Rinsed spirit of me, washed for this departure,
   Takes off adroitly to its atmosphere.

And here's that blue glove on a railing's tip
   Where iron, frost and wool make partnership
Of animal and elements and blue –
   Lost little glove, I still remember you.

You do not fit my hand now, nor can I fit
   My world with life; nor my mouth match its spit;
My tongue, my words; my eyes, the things they see.
   My head is upside down in memory.

A child walks to his mother, right hand bare
   And hidden in his coat, then follows her
Inside, his gloved hand on the banister,
   His right hand on his heart, remaining there.

My pulse beats backwards to a street in winter –
   Blue first perceived, that I now disinter
Blue out of blue where life and childhood crossed:
   Five blue wool-fingers waving in the frost.

Douglas Dunn

The philosopher stops work to look out the window

Who was I to deny a headstrong balloon
simple delight? Its helium will was
to make for the sun; I watched it recede
from the lanes where I played.

Sometimes in there, I'd mutter my name
over and over till meaning leaked from the sound
leaving it saggy like the skin of balloons.
It no longer felt mine! People chant
over their dead in the East, mother once said.
I knew why: 'after you die you become a baby again'.

But these afternoons I spend shaking my head
as if it contained a sample of life,
and the aim? To separate
meaningful curds from ineffable whey.
But today, look what's stopping the traffic
down on the street: an unfettered balloon!

Kathleen Jamie

Winter-Time

Monday, at the gloamin',
  I saw a reid reid lowe,
Whaur tinker fouk wull ne'er set fit,
  Far ben in the ghaisty howe;
And yon that gaed ahint me
  Was nae sheda o' my ain.
It's eerie fa' the nichts
  Aifter Marti'mas is gane.

Twa e'en as bleck as howlets,
  A week past Marti'mas,
Glowered ower the new-lit can'els
  Frae oot the luikin'-glass;
And Three cam' creepin' doon the loan
  On Thursday in the mirk,
Whase shoon was wrocht in yon far toon
  That ne'er had Cross nor kirk.

I hard the elfin pipers
  Sae witchin', sweet an' sma'
On Sabbath wi' the warld asleep;
  They wiled my hert awa'.
They stilled the soughin' o' the burn –
  O, tae a lanesome lass
There's eerie freits on ilka road,
  When bye is Marti'mas.

Marion Angus

The Educators

In their
limousines the
teachers come: by
hundreds. O the
square is
blackened with dark suits, with grave
scholastic faces. They
wait to be summoned.
These are the
educators, the
father-figures. O you could
warm with love for the firm lips, the
responsible foreheads. Their
ties are strongly set, between their collars. They
pass with dignity the exasperation of waiting.

A
bell rings. They turn. On the
wide steps my
dwarf is standing, both hands raised. He
cackles with laughter. Welcome, he cries, welcome
to our elaborate Palace. It is indeed. He
is tumbling in cartwheels over the steps. The
teachers turn to each other their grave faces.

With
a single grab they have him up by the shoulders. They
dismantle him. Limbs, O
limbs and delicate organs, limbs and
guts, eyes, the tongue, the
lobes of the brain, glands; tonsils, several
eyes, limbs, the tongue,
a kidney, pants, livers, more
kidneys, limbs, the tongue
pass from hand to hand, in their serious hands. He is
utterly gone. Wide
crumbling steps.

They
return to their cars. They
drive off smoothly, without disorder;
watching the road.

David Black

31

At School

Millions and millions of stars,
hundreds and hundreds of countries.

And there is old Miss Twiss
going on about squares.

Nothing but dust in the room.
And names on the desks.

Iain Crichton Smith

This Nor That

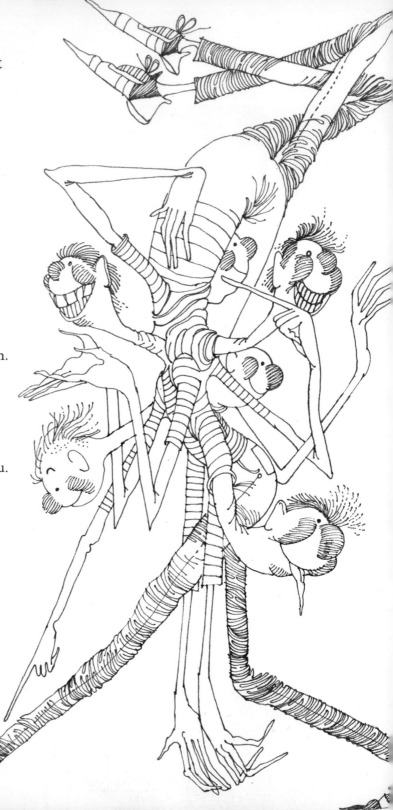

Am I either?
I am neither.
I am neither
This nor that.

Do you claim me?
You can't same me.
I am neither
Round or flat.

Are you singing?
Then I'm listening.
Are you looking?
I'll look too.

You forgetting?
I'll remember.
You for going?
I'll help you through.

Want a burden?
Upsadaisy!
Need a rest?
Tut tut tut.

Want a fight?
I'll stand behind you.
Want a kiss?
I'll stand in front.

I'm kind of going,
Kind of staying,
Kind of no-ing,
Kind of yea-ing.

More exactly
What I'm saying:
I am neither
This nor that.

Alan Jackson

Spaceman

I think I'll be a spaceman
And trevel to the mune
To poke aboot the craters
And see what I can fin'

They say it's fou o diamonds.
Gowd and siller ore;
I'll lade them in my spaceship
Till I hae quite a store.

Then I'll come hame a rich man
And dander up the street
Noddin my fancy helmet
To ilka sowl I meet.

J.K. Annand

35

At tea-time

Comin hame fae school aince I met
a spleet-new corpse, a square-made, grey-heidit man,
a workin man; on the kerb stane
next the Clydesdale bank.
Bleed was growin near his left lug.
His mate knelt ower'm, syne lookit up
and said 'He's deid. I'll phone the doctor.'
                              It was a waste o time.
His pump had stoppit for good.
Jist aboot half past fower in the aifterneen he drappit oot
o time and history into naethinhness in his workin claes.
I lookit doun and couldna come up
wi onything that could tak the measure
o the man, or mak ony sense o his new sleep.

Three o's had some work humphin his cement
into the manager's office. A ton wecht he was!
He'd hae gotten nae tea that nicht.

Alastair Mackie

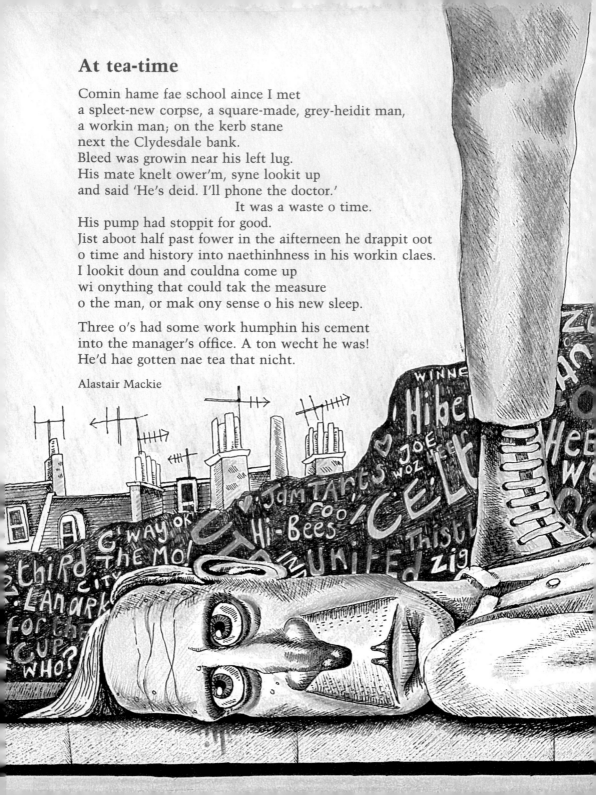

Little By Little

My chum Eric was well-behaved,
spoke English properly, and always said please.
His mother wore a critical look
where I was concerned. True, I was depraved
enough to pick scabs from my knees,
speak with my mouth full, and seldom took

her hints about washing my hands.
My mother offered Eric as a model for me,
in place of the rough boys at the end of our street
with whom I rode whooping into the bad-lands,
played Cowboys-and-Indians, swung from a tree
like Tarzan, or went without shoes on my feet.

One afternoon, in a new blazer bought
that very Saturday, Eric fell
splash into the Park pond, scaring
all the tadpoles we might have caught.
He ran home feeling quite unwell
and told his Mum I'd pushed him in. Swearing

innocence was all to no avail.
His mother said I'd lost his Hornby train,
taught him rude words and where babies came from.
No, he wouldn't be going to the Park to sail
his boat and never would play with me again –
and she fully intended to tell my Mum.

Thus I learned how life is quite unfair,
there is no justice, and all is care
and woe. Some get a better share
of good things; others get the blame.

I saw Eric yesterday. He looks just the same,
running and wet, and still missing his train!

Ken Morrice

When I leave school

When I leave school I want to be
a captain on the raging sea

or a pilot in a plane
or a scientist with a brain

or a player like Dalglish
or a swimmer like a fish.

Actually what I'll be
I'll live at No 23

Renton St with seven weans,
and a lot of smoke from passing trains.

Iain Crichton Smith

Small Boy and Lighthouse

You, little rugged boy without seat to your trousers,
Your senses pinned to a string, your boots hanging over the harbour,
Remember, when you are older, the green sea rocking,
The black sea knocking the ships;
Remember the taut ropes groaning, the lift and suck of the hulls,
The smell of the herring boxes, the bright scales stuck to the jetty,
The sequin scales on your hands, that you wipe on your trousers.
Remember the swearing gulls and the gannets diving,
The cormorants crucified; remember the rust-caked dredger,
The coal truck swung from a crane, and the dust, and the thunder.
Remember the huge night also, with zigzag on slow water
Of yellow and red lights tangling, and how from darkness
A white flash, sharp as a pin, pulled out an island.

Sydney Tremayne

Sea Ballad

A waukrife weidie on the sand
  Wes walkan aa her lane
And met the ghaist o her ain man
  Wydan up frae the main.

'Cauld is your bed the nicht,' quo she,
  'Amang the seals and fish.'
'It's naither cauld nor het,' said he,
  'But muckle as ane wad wish.'

'Gin it's no cauld,' the weidie cried,
  'Ye maun be leesome lane.'
'That's juist a tale,' the ghaist replied:
  'I'm never on my ain.

'I've neebors frae the warld wide
  Wi endless tales in store,
And swans and selkies frae the tide
  Are hertsome wi their lore.'

'Hou daft are we,' in tears said she,
  'Whan we bewail the brave
And them in sic braw companie
  In the land aneath the wave!'

'A truer word ye never spak,'
  He said, but sair grat she,
Whan in a blink he turned his back
  And santit in the sea.

A.D. Mackie

Wave/Rock

wave
wave
wave
wave rock
wave rock
wave rock
rock
rock
rock
rock
rock

Ian Hamilton Finlay

Hungry Waters
For a little boy at Linlithgow

The auld men o' the sea
Wi' their daberlack hair
Ha'e dackered the coasts
O' the country fell sair.

They gobble owre cas'les,
Chow mountains to san';
Or lang they'll eat up
The haill o' the lan'.

Lickin' their white lips
An' yowlin' for mair,
The auld men o' the sea
Wi' their daberlack hair.

Hugh MacDiarmid

The Years of the Crocodile
A Dirge

In the years o the maytree
The hevins were bricht
In the years o the crocodile
Nicht wantan licht.

In the years o the lily
I loed wiout loss
In the years o the crocodile
Tosspots I toss.

In the years o the rose
I read aa the bukes
In the years o the crocodile
I lossit my looks.

In the years o solsequium
I secutit the sun
In the years o the crocodile
I sat on my bum.

In the years o the vine
I'd a horse for the wish
In the years o the crocodile
I drank like a fish.

In the years o the lotus
I wore a lum hat
In the years o the crocodile
I sat doun and grat.

O the tears o the crocodile
Fill the Waters o Leith
And the glent o the gourmand
Sheens on his teeth.

O the tears o the crocodile
Greit for us aa
Wi a grin o content
He lowsens his jaws.

Sydney Goodsir Smith

46

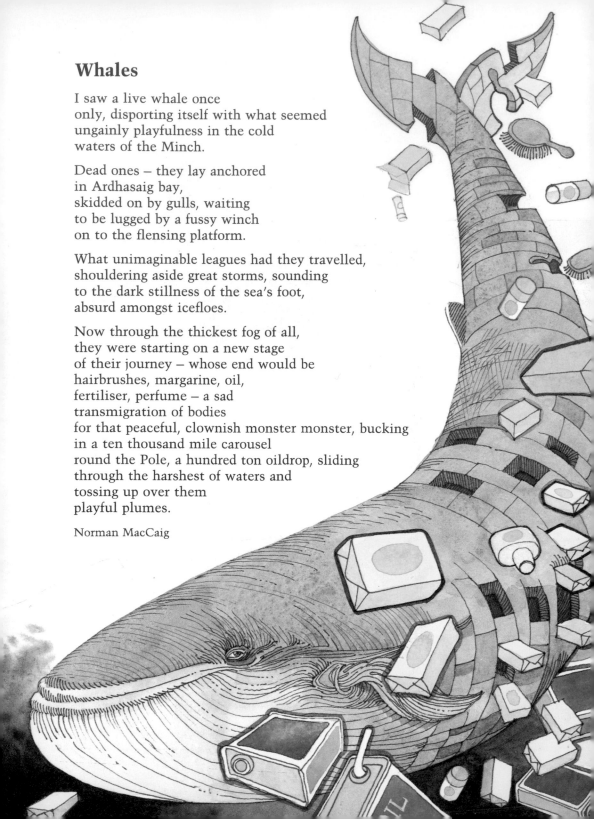

Whales

I saw a live whale once
only, disporting itself with what seemed
ungainly playfulness in the cold
waters of the Minch.

Dead ones – they lay anchored
in Ardhasaig bay,
skidded on by gulls, waiting
to be lugged by a fussy winch
on to the flensing platform.

What unimaginable leagues had they travelled,
shouldering aside great storms, sounding
to the dark stillness of the sea's foot,
absurd amongst icefloes.

Now through the thickest fog of all,
they were starting on a new stage
of their journey – whose end would be
hairbrushes, margarine, oil,
fertiliser, perfume – a sad
transmigration of bodies
for that peaceful, clownish monster monster, bucking
in a ten thousand mile carousel
round the Pole, a hundred ton oildrop, sliding
through the harshest of waters and
tossing up over them
playful plumes.

Norman MacCaig

Submarine

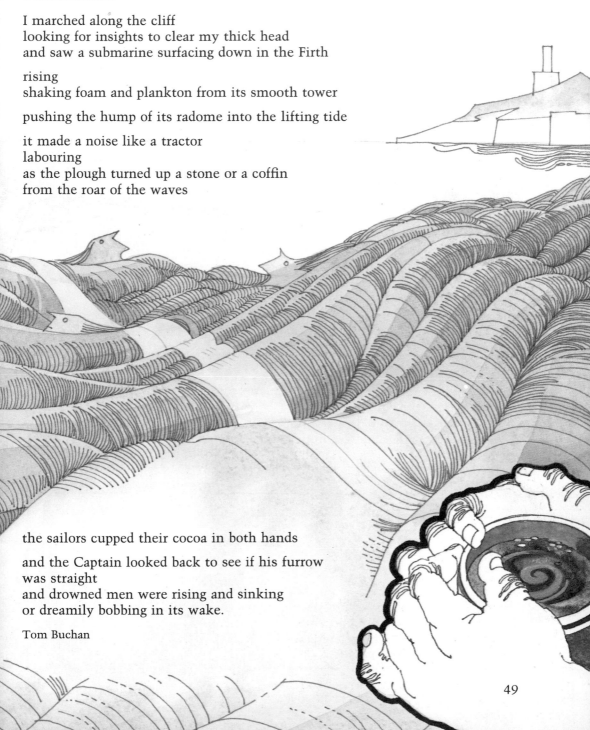

I marched along the cliff
looking for insights to clear my thick head
and saw a submarine surfacing down in the Firth

rising
shaking foam and plankton from its smooth tower

pushing the hump of its radome into the lifting tide

it made a noise like a tractor
labouring
as the plough turned up a stone or a coffin
from the roar of the waves

the sailors cupped their cocoa in both hands

and the Captain looked back to see if his furrow
was straight
and drowned men were rising and sinking
or dreamily bobbing in its wake.

Tom Buchan

49

The Clown
[A Surrealist Fable]

Drifting too near the Roznian coast
a giant egg got spat ashore
like many a ship before it, lost
between the teething breakers' roar.

From out the shattered shell, a clown
cocooned in boots, loose whey-faced clothes
and straggled orange hair, pulled down
his battered hat and bulbous nose,

then scrambled up the Roznian cliffs
and, though he didn't know it, reached
where neither jokes nor *buts* and *ifs*
were tolerated, since they breached

the ways of an omniscient State
whose citizens by law were free,
though individuals didn't rate
in such enforced equality.

A farmer, solemn as his cow,
saw him. They gloomed the time of day
till, round a deferential bow,
he somersaulted through the hay.

A village politician talked
of hardship for the common good.
Up popped a mirrored clown who mocked
his gestures, emptied thought from food.

Next, waggling hips with mimed guitar,
an anguished pop star he became,
the moment's idol; but a star
who sloughed away his instant fame.

A serious short-sighted girl
called him her hero. Jesting, he
slowed down her fancy's amorous whirl
with pity, proferred tenderly.

Though clowns pretend to broken hearts,
marriage becomes a frozen pose
when there are still a thousand parts
to prank, a self to re-compose.

50

In each community he travelled
he shocked the posters preaching truth
as State-decreed; with doubt unravelled
their numbing hold on age and youth.

Through that unsmiling land he tumbled,
tearing the shadows from its rules
till some folk questioned why they stumbled.
Was laughter only fit for fools?

The havoc that he caused increased.
Goose-stepping soldiers, trained to kill,
felt less inspired to be deceased
defending dogma's mindless will.

He parodied official spies,
reversing secret information;
turned good to bad, put truth for lies,
thus damaging the processed nation.

Its President pronounced him treason:
This dangerous clown must be suppressed,
or subjects might begin to reason
and wonder why the State knows best.

So Roznian party chiefs declared
humour a capital offence,
since everything that's safely shared
must be obediently dense.

Still fooling when condemned to die,
they dragged him to a secret place
where, though he never asked them why,
they stripped the paint that caked his face,

the garments that his ways had worn,
and threw him back into the sea.
The membrane of his laughter torn,
he sank and drowned, like you or me.

Maurice Lindsay

The Loch Ness Monster

Sometimes at night when the wind blows hard
the Loch Ness monster is lonely
for his extinct contemporaries
the warm flying fox and the luscious algae

so too in the long silent hours when the wind blows
(the black water closing over my head)
I am lonely for you my extinct love
pinioned down there in the strata

'I love you' I cry –
but you cannot weep or move your head

and I am terrified I shall not be near you again
until the rocks are broken
and our dead dust is blown out into space.

Tom Buchan

THE BOAT'S BLUEPRINT

water

Ian Hamilton Finlay

The Talk of the Headlands

Says Ebbing Point to Laggan Head:
'Where do they watch their nets to spread
on the black lifting of the sea,
that laid their homeward course on me?'

'When the sun stoops and leaves the sky
the loch lies dead, with not a cry
or torch to mark from far or near.
It leaves me lonely, watching here.'

Says Laggan Head across the bight:
'What sounds the men must rienge to-night,
not Holy Isle or Ailsa know,
who flashed farewell and saw them go.'

'They search dark seas they never kent,
seeking out death, ill-rested, spent;
yet sweet it drones aye in their ear,
the swell that breaks upon us here.'

George Campbell Hay

Seaweed

A myriad tides have foamed
  And myriad moons been lit
While this brown weed was made
  And sea-stones clothed in it.

All time, and this vast world's
  Strong tides, sun, moon, and air
Have laboured to display
  Eternal autumn there!

William Jeffrey

waterwheels in

Ian Hamilton Finlay

56

Cart Wheels

At twelve years old I drove a sweating pair
of Clydesdales down the edge of standing corn.
Five times my age, old Jock beside me there
worked the tiltboard and cursed me for a born
fool, if I let them walk out from the edge
or snagged the corn-divider in the hedge.

Taught me to harness horses and drive carts,
to curry-comb while hissing through slack lips,
to work a ricklifter and all the arts
that rural pride from the dumb city keeps.
I'd imitate his ploughman walk and grin,
wear strings below my knee-joints just like him.

Torn from these agricultural concerns,
ten times Jock's wages in the city hubbub
I found quite early on that I could earn,
and live within a comfortable suburb
where painted cartwheels have become folk-art
and of some prissy garden form a part.

Red, green and blue they stand at gable walls
or are converted into garden gates;
some, small enough, may stand inside a hall,
a conversation piece for dinner dates.
Jock would have spat, and coarsely cursed such tricks
and split the lot up into kindling sticks.

William Neill

The Wooden Curlew

She was the extra decoy,
the one who looked different
to make the others credible.
She served her purpose
in the first hour of October light
amid the guns, the wounded splashing
and the black ripples
of the swimming dogs.

As daylight grew stronger
the gunfire tailed away.
Its sharp smoke slipped from
the hanging willow branches
while the men packed up their gear
into the green Range Rover
and drove off. She was left,
forgotten in the lee of a birch root.
She wintered there with weathering paint,
attracting real wildfowl to the safety
of the shallows by the empty hides.

The March floods lifted her
from her black nest in the withered reeds.
Slower and heavier with the winter's weight
of water in her frost-sprung grain,
she bobbed across the lake
and in the false dawn saw
the headlights cross the misty ridge
and park beside the water.
She saw the men launch the punt
and lay the mallard decoys
in a floating line.
There was no wooden curlew
to make them real. Still,
uncertain of what she had become,
she kept her distance from the slanting guns.

Robin Bell

'great'

great
tae be hunners o burds
an sit in trees
an wash yer nebs
in rainy leaves

Alan Jackson

The Eagle, Crow, and Shepherd
A Fable

Beneath the horror of a rock,
A shepherd careless fed his flock.
Souse from its top an eagle came,
And seiz'd upon a sporting lamb;
Its tender sides his talons tear,
And bear it bleating thro' the air.

This was discover'd by a crow,
Who hopp'd upon the plain below.
'Yon ram,' says he, 'becomes my prey'
And, mounting, hastens to the fray:
Lights on his back – when lo, ill-luck!
He in the fleece entangled stuck:
He spreads his wings, but can't get free,
Struggling in vain for liberty.

The shepherd soon the captive spies,
And soon he seizes on the prize.
His children curious crowd around,
And ask what strange fowl he has found?

'My sons,' said he, 'warn'd by this wretch,
Attempt no deed above your reach:
An eagle not an hour ago,
He's now content to be a crow.'

Michael Bruce

61

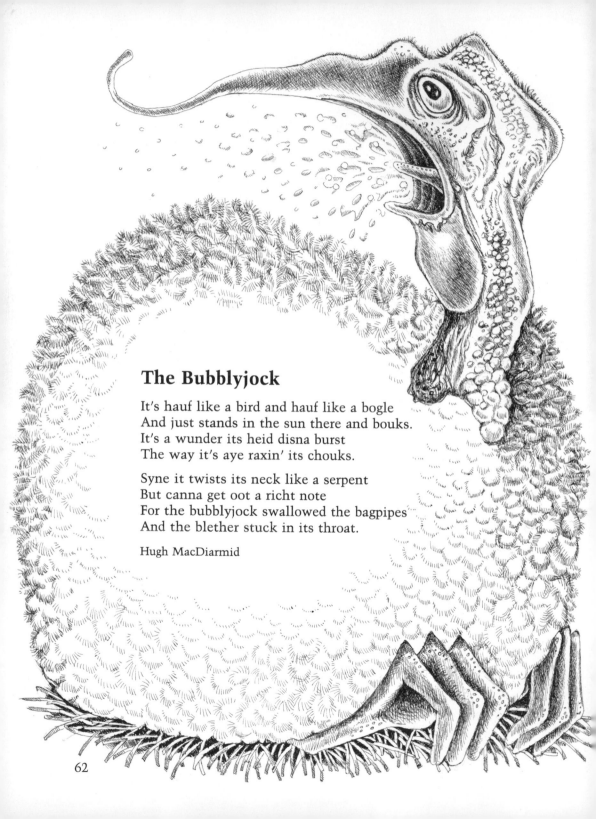

The Bubblyjock

It's hauf like a bird and hauf like a bogle
And just stands in the sun there and bouks.
It's a wunder its heid disna burst
The way it's aye raxin' its chouks.

Syne it twists its neck like a serpent
But canna get oot a richt note
For the bubblyjock swallowed the bagpipes
And the blether stuck in its throat.

Hugh MacDiarmid

62

The Eagle

Between two mighty hills a sheer
    Abyss – far down in the ravine
    A thread-like torrent and a screen
Of oaks like shrubs – and one doth rear
    A dry scarp'd peak above all sound
    Save windy voices wailing round:

At sunrise here, in proud disdain
The eagle scans his vast domain.

William Sharp

The Owl

As slowly as the moon he woke
and raised his amber eyes;
he waited in his hollow oak
till starlight pricked the sky.

He glided through the frosty air
and far beneath he saw
the rustling woodlands unaware
of unsheathed beak and claw.

And you who work and eat by day,
lie still in your beds tonight;
the owl is listening for his prey
and his wings are whispering white.

Robin Bell

UFO

I held the lead pencil
by the sharp end
between left forefinger and thumb
and let the black ant run along it

Halfway I changed my grip
to the blunt end
between right forefinger and thumb

The short-sighted ant
stopped at the sharp lead
waving two antennae
into the void

spiralled round the pencil
between a blue sky
and no earth
and ran back along the pencil

Halfway I changed my grip
to the sharp lead
between left index finger and thumb

The black ant stopped
at the blunt end
waved two antennae
into the void
marooned on a green pencil in space

When my pencil touched down
the ant hurried off
to report her voyage
to where God shines by day
and they added this UFO
to the list
in the office of the flying ants

The talk between antennae
continued for weeks
whether God or the Devil
in the seventh dimension
controlled these phenomena

William Montgomerie

GREAT
FROG
RACE

A FLO P

Ian Hamilton Finlay

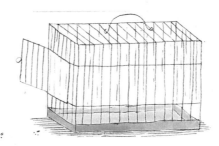

Pigsny-pogsny

I called her fig, I called her pog;
But never pigsny-pogsny.

I styled her lambkin-nibblybits
But never pigsny-pogsny.

She answered to my furrybun
And to my choolyburger:

To diddly-squeak and pussy-dear;
Yet never pigsny-pogsny.

She must have gone as fluffychops
I hope I called her poplet.

She never would have left, my mouse,
If I'd called her pigsny-pogsny.

Alastair Fowler

Blind Horse

He snuffles towards
pouches of water in the grass
and doesn't drink
when he finds them.

He twitches listlessly at
sappy grass stems and stands
stone still, his hanging head
caricatured with a scribble
of green whiskers.

Sometimes that head swings high,
ears cock – and he stares
down a long sound,
he stares and whinnies
for what never comes.

His eyes never close,
not in the heat of the day
when his leather lip droops and
he wears blinkers of flies.

At any time of the night
you hear him in his dark field
stamp the ground, stamp
the world down, waiting impatiently
for the light to break.

Norman MacCaig

71

The Horses

Barely a twelvemonth after
The seven days war that put the world to sleep,
Late in the evening the strange horses came.
By then we had made our covenant with silence,
But in the first few days it was so still
We listened to our breathing and were afraid.
On the second day
The radios failed; we turned the knobs; no answer.
On the third day a warship passed us, heading north,
Dead bodies piled on the deck. On the sixth day
A plane plunged over us into the sea. Thereafter
Nothing. The radios dumb;
And still they stand in corners of our kitchens,
And stand, perhaps, turned on, in a million rooms
All over the world. But now if they should speak,
If on a sudden they should speak again,
If on the stroke of noon a voice should speak,
We would not listen, we would not let it bring
That old bad world that swallowed its children quick
At one great gulp. We would not have it again.
Sometimes we think of the nations lying asleep,
Curled blindly in impenetrable sorrow,
And then the thought confounds us with its strangeness.
The tractors lie about our fields; at evening
They look like dank sea-monsters couched and waiting.
We leave them where they are and let them rust:
'They'll moulder away and be like other loam'.
We make our oxen drag our rusty ploughs,
Long laid aside. We have gone back
Far past our fathers' land.

And then, that evening
Late in the summer the strange horses came.
We heard a distant tapping on the road,
A deepening drumming; it stopped, went on again
And at the corner changed to hollow thunder.
We saw the heads
Like a wild wave charging and were afraid.
We had sold our horses in our fathers' time
To buy new tractors. Now they were strange to us
As fabulous steeds set on an ancient shield
Or illustrations in a book of knights.
We did not dare go near them. Yet they waited,
Stubborn and shy, as if they had been sent
By an old command to find our whereabouts
And that long-lost archaic companionship.
In the first moment we had never a thought
That they were creatures to be owned and used.
Among them were some half-a-dozen colts
Dropped in some wilderness of the broken world,
Yet new as if they had come from their own Eden.
Since then they have pulled our ploughs and borne our loads,
But that free servitude still can pierce our hearts.
Our life is changed; their coming our beginning.

Edwin Muir

The Raiders

Last night a wind from Lammermoor came roaring up the glen,
With the tramp of trooping horses and the laugh of reckless men,
And struck a mailed hand on the gate and cried in rebel glee:
'Come forth, Come forth, my Borderer, and ride the March with me!'

I said, 'Oh! Wind of Lammermoor, the night's too dark to ride,
And all the men that fill the glen are ghosts of men that died!
The floods are down in Bowmont Burn, the moss is fetlock-deep;
Go back, wild Wind of Lammermoor, to Lauderdale – and sleep!'

Out spoke the Wind of Lammermoor, 'We know the road right well,
The road that runs by Kale and Jed across the Carter Fell.
There is no man of all the men in this grey troop of mine
But blind might ride the Borderside from Teviothead to Tyne!'

The horses fretted on their bits and pawed the flints to fire,
The riders swung them to the South full-faced to their desire;
'Come!' said the Wind from Lammermoor, and spoke full scornfully,
'Have ye no pride to mount and ride your fathers' road with me?'

A roan horse to the gate they led, foam-flecked and travelled far,
A snorting roan that tossed his head and flashed his forehead star;
There came the sound of clashing steel and hoof-tramp up the glen.
  And two by two we cantered through, a troop of ghostly men!

·   ·   ·

I know not if the farms we fired are burned to ashes yet!
I know not if the stirks grew tired before the stars were set!
I only know that late last night when Northern winds blew free,
A troop of men rode up the glen and brought a horse for me!

Will H. Ogilvie

Hal o' the Wynd

Hal o' the Wynd he taen the field
Alang be the skinklin Tay:
And he hackit doun the men o' Chattan;
Or was it the men o' Kay?

Whan a' was owre he dichted his blade
And steppit awa richt douce
To draik his drouth in the Skinners' Vennel
At clapperin Clemmy's house.

Hal o' the Wynd had monie a bairn;
And bairns' bairns galore
Wha wud speer about the bluidy battle
And what it was fochten for.

'Guid-faith! my dawties, I never kent;
But yon was a dirlin day
Whan I hackit doun the men o' Chattan;
Or was it the men o' Kay?'

William Soutar

Hopes

October winds are over the Lammermuirs,
The gecking grouse are whirring about their slopes
   And meadow-pipits tsip and flutter
   hither and thither in charms, in flocklets.

The autumn glens are tinted with reds and browns,
With golds and greens and purples, with mauves and grays
   Where sheep, among the heather scattered,
   Litter the ground like discarded papers.

And here in Hopes the burn is meand'ring down
The hillside, as it did ere the Bruce was born,
   Its voice a simple, quiet brattle
   Scarcely perceptible in the stillness.

What peace the glen affords us this golden day!
What gifts of solace for the tormented heart,
   What beauty, undemanded, given,
   Lavished on us by indulgent Nature!

In such a scene it's hard to believe that folk,
So blessed by Mother Earth with her paradise,
   Should even now prepare her murder,
   Hoping to cling to their own mad systems.

It isn't much to hope that our human race,
The shepherd of all creatures of Earthly birth,
   Win lasting peace for all our kindred
   Here in this garden of all the planets.

It isn't much to hope that the dogs of war
Who steal the children's bread from their hungry mouths,
   Should be put down, or tamed, so human
   Beings survive here in peace and plenty.

Tom Scott

Brigs o' Braid

[a ballad of a highway robbery, 1814]

'O, Davie Loch, get up and gae,
The cock is crawing cheerily,
The Biggar haugh's like blossomed slae,
November winds blaw drearily.'

As he rade ower bleak Roslin Muir
The sun was set and mune was nane.
It was as mirk as midnight oor
Atween the Buck and Camus Stane.

Doon in the dell at Brigs o' Braid
The houlets hoot, the freshets fuss,
But Davie Loch is no afraid
Until he's near the auld thorn buss.

For there he sees a fremit wight,
The glint o' a pistol butt sees he.
'Can yez plaze to tell me the hour o' night?'
'It's sax o'clock, as near's may be.'

They hae grippet Davie by the boot
And dragged him frae his auld grey mare.
They hae kneed him doon by the auld thorn root
And brak his ribs and mauled him sair.

They hae riped his pooch and stown his purse,
Wi the pistol rapped him ower the heid.
They hae taen their wey oot ower the furs
And left puir Davie Loch for deid.

Afore the Tron has chappit ten
To Edinburgh the word's gane roun;
The sheriff has sent twa score o' men
Wi batons black to scour the toun.

They searched ilk Bow and Bristo howff,
They raiked the Coogate ilka pen,
Till at the dawin drear and dowf
In the West Port they fund their men.

'Come oot Tam Kelly and Harry O'Neil!
Surrender in King George's name!
Come oot in the name o' the muckle deil
That a' the toun may ken your shame.'

The trial is set, the judges glower,
But witness o' the crime was nane
For the deed was done at darklin hour
When Davie Loch was a' alane.

'D'yer ken your purse, noo, Davie, my man?'
For a purse was fund in Kelly's breeks,
'I ken it like the back o' my haun,
It bears the mark o' my wife's three steeks.'

They hae set twa stanes in the Plewlands Lea,
On the brae below the Brigs o' Braid.
In ilk stane sits a gallows tree,
And it's there the last accoont was paid.

Forbes Macgregor

End of a cold night

The pond has closed its frozen eyelid,
The grass clump clenched its frozen claws.
The sky wheels like a millstone dropping grains
Of frost through air drawn thin and clear as glass.

The moon lies bleaching on the hedges.
A cock crows thinly and far away
– And a spell is broken; suddenly Time scratches
The hour on its box and up flares a new day.

Norman MacCaig

The Guy

In orange sweater, and blue, bulging jeans,
Footless, with one leg severed at the knee,
   Our stuffed guy slumps beside the wall.
And what will happen to him should appal,

Surely, if we considered what it means:
The scorching of the flames, indecent glee,
   And children screeching round the blaze,
Their faces dark as crystal in its glaze.

Grey-faced, and green-haired, with newspaper guts,
The guy should represent our deepest fears.
   But something hampers, and his lean
Against the wall seems casual, and obscene.

The Roman candle quivers, banger phutts,
And sparklers fill the sky with fiery spears.
   The witch must die, the witch must burn,
The Catherine wheel revolves. When will they learn?

This eloquent young bruiser, punk and shrill,
Unspeakable in dress, and stuffed with words,
   In two days time, charred black as news,
Will filter into ash below those yews.

I watch him like a hunter from the hill
And walk through cracking brush, flushing the birds.
   The day has come, the bonfire's laid.
I dig a grave for rockets with my spade.

George MacBeth

81

War-Dream

Now the earth has stopped rising
and falling he is carrying her from
the rubble she wears a print dress thin
pale hair she could be
the child we don't have he
is weeping with gratitude shc's
still alive he hasn't yet seen
the deep blue cave pressed
pressed into one side of her head

Andrew Greig

Precisely To Scale

The trunks of great Brazilian balsa trees
Are floated down the Amazon for struts
Of model aeroplanes, which Andrew cuts
   Delicately, on his knees,
Over his mother's borrowed pastry board.
A Spitfire's lovely skeleton grows in white wood.

Next week he'll fly it by the reservoir
With Martin (reading *Eagle* on the bed).
   This week's centre spread
Is given over to a Jaguar,
A D-type racer. Martin, feeling skittish,
Bets a Ferrari's faster. Ferraris are not British

   So how can that be so?
They wrestle. Martin loses. Being such
A little squit, he doesn't mind too much,
Just hooks band-aided specs back on. They go
Down to the stream and get well scratched and muddy
Collecting newts for Martin's fishtank. Nature study

Is Martin's passion. Andrew likes it too,
   Though there are sure to be
Ructions about the state of his jersey
(Martin being common and some sort of jew).
Look, that's a heron. Ain't it marvellous!
Andrew doesn't see it, but pretends he does.

They spend most summer afternoons together
Mucking around and doing nothing nearly.
   Inseparable really,
Through the sweet, langorous boredom of hot weather.
Mostly they talk, and Martin likes to swear.
Though Andrew's mother winces, Andrew doesn't care.

But how can Martin not believe in God
And Jesus? Surely anyone can see
The Bible's written true as history.
   Martin won't give a sod
For that — his universe began because
· A cloud of gas went bang, and that's the way it was.

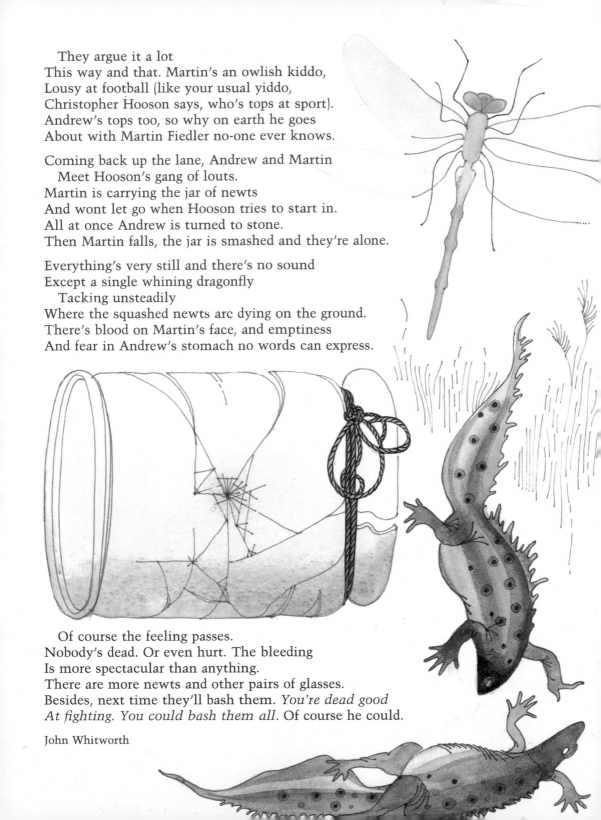

They argue it a lot
This way and that. Martin's an owlish kiddo,
Lousy at football (like your usual yiddo,
Christopher Hooson says, who's tops at sport).
Andrew's tops too, so why on earth he goes
About with Martin Fiedler no-one ever knows.

Coming back up the lane, Andrew and Martin
    Meet Hooson's gang of louts.
Martin is carrying the jar of newts
And wont let go when Hooson tries to start in.
All at once Andrew is turned to stone.
Then Martin falls, the jar is smashed and they're alone.

Everything's very still and there's no sound
Except a single whining dragonfly
    Tacking unsteadily
Where the squashed newts arc dying on the ground.
There's blood on Martin's face, and emptiness
And fear in Andrew's stomach no words can express.

Of course the feeling passes.
Nobody's dead. Or even hurt. The bleeding
Is more spectacular than anything.
There are more newts and other pairs of glasses.
Besides, next time they'll bash them. *You're dead good
At fighting. You could bash them all*. Of course he could.

John Whitworth

Think On Me

When I no more behold thee,
    Think on me!
By all thine eyes have told me,
    Think on me!
When hearts are lightest,
When eyes are brightest,
When griefs are slightest,
    Think on me!

In all thine hours of gladness,
    Think on me!
If e'er I soothed thy sadness,
    Think on me!
When foes are by thee,
When woes are nigh thee,
When friends all fly thee,
    Think on me!

When thou hast none to cheer thee,
    Think on me!
When no fond heart is near thee,
    Think on me!
When lonely sighing,
O'er pleasures flying,
When hope is dying,
    Think on me!

Lady John Scott

The Two Brothers

There were twa brethren in the north,
   They went to the school thegither;
The one unto the other said,
   'Will you try a warsle afore?'

They warsled up, they warsled down,
   Till Sir John fell to the ground,
And there was a knife in Sir Willie's pouch,
   Gied him a deadlie wound.

'Oh brither dear, take me on your back,
   Carry me to yon burn clear,
And wash the blood from off my wound,
   And it will bleed nae mair.'

He took him up upon his back,
   Carried him to yon burn clear,
And wash'd the blood from off his wound,
   But aye it bled the mair.

'Oh brither dear, take me on your back,
   Carry me to yon kirkyard,
And dig a grave baith wide and deep,
   And lay my body there.'

He's ta'en him up upon his back,
    Carried him to yon kirkyard,
And dug a grave baith deep and wide,
    And laid his body there.

'But what will I say to my father dear,
    Gin he chance to say, Willie, whar's John?'
'Oh say that he's to England gone,
    To buy him a cask of wine.'

'And what will I say to my mother dear,
    Gin she chance to say, Willie, whar's John?'
'Oh say that he's to England gone,
    To buy her a new silk gown.'

'And what will I say to my sister dear,
    Gin she chance to say, Willie, whar's John?'
'Oh say that he's to England gone,
    To buy her a wedding ring.'

But what will I say to her you lo'e dear,
    Gin she cry, Why tarries my John?'
'Oh tell her I lie in Kirk-land fair,
    And home again will never come.'

Anonymous

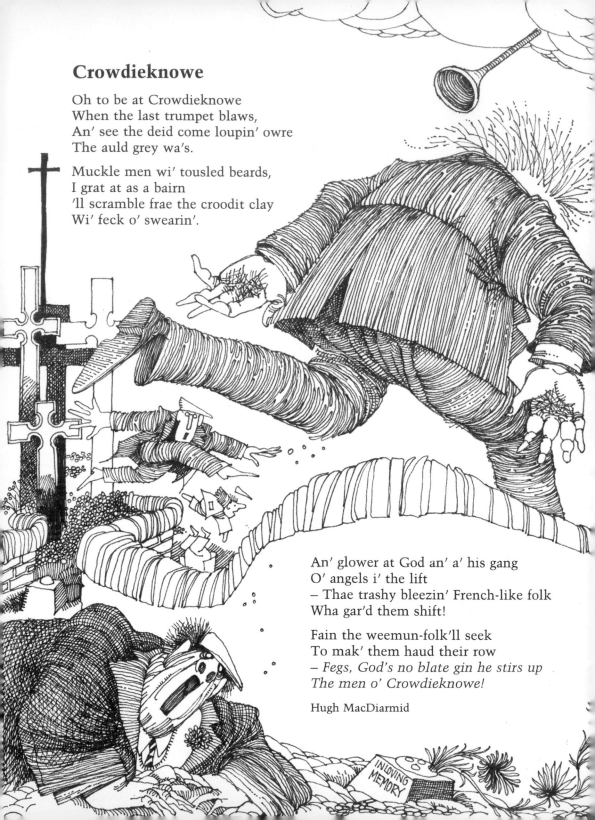

Crowdieknowe

Oh to be at Crowdieknowe
When the last trumpet blaws,
An' see the deid come loupin' owre
The auld grey wa's.

Muckle men wi' tousled beards,
I grat at as a bairn
'll scramble frae the croodit clay
Wi' feck o' swearin'.

An' glower at God an' a' his gang
O' angels i' the lift
– Thae trashy bleezin' French-like folk
Wha gar'd them shift!

Fain the weemun-folk'll seek
To mak' them haud their row
– *Fegs, God's no blate gin he stirs up*
The men o' Crowdieknowe!

Hugh MacDiarmid

The Flowers of the Forest

I've heard the lilting at our yowe-milking,
　　Lasses a-lilting before the dawn o' day;
But now they are moaning on ilka green loaning:
　　'The Flowers of the Forest are a' wede away.'

At buchts, in the morning, nae blythe lads are scorning;
　　The lasses are lonely, and dowie, and wae;
Nae daffin', nae gabbin', but sighing and sabbing:
　　Ilk ane lifts her leglen, and hies her away.

In hairst, at the shearing, nae youths now are jeering,
　　The bandsters are lyart, and runkled and grey;
At fair or at preaching, nae wooing, nae fleeching:
　　The Flowers of the Forest are a' wede away.

At e'en, in the gloaming, nae swankies are roaming
　　'Bout stacks wi' the lasses at bogle to play,
But ilk ane sits drearie, lamenting her dearie:
　　The Flowers of the Florest are a' wede away.

Dule and wae for the order set our lads to the Border;
　　The English, for ance, by guile wan the day;
The Flowers of the Forest, that foucht aye the foremost,
　　The prime o' our land, are cauld in the clay.

We'll hear nae mair lilting at our yowe-milking,
　　Women and bairns are heartless and wae;
Sighing and moaning on ilka green loaning:
　　'The Flowers of the Forest are a' wede away.'

Jane Elliot

Lochinvar

[from Marmion]

O, young Lochinvar is come out of the west,
Through all the wide Border his steed was the best;
And save his good broadsword he weapons had none,
He rode all unarm'd, and he rode all alone.
So faithful in love, and so dauntless in war,
There never was knight like the young Lochinvar.

He staid not for brake, and he stopp'd not for stone,
He swam the Eske river where ford there was none;
But ere he alighted at Netherby gate,
The bride had consented, the gallant came late:
For a laggard in love, and a dastard in war,
Was to wed the fair Ellen of brave Lochinvar.

So boldly he enter'd the Netherby Hall,
Among the bride's-men, and kinsmen, and brothers, and all:
Then spoke the bride's father, his hand on his sword,
(For the poor craven bridegroom said never a word,)
'O come ye in peace here, or come ye in war,
Or to dance at our bridal, young Lord Lochinvar?'

'I long woo'd your daughter, my suit you denied; —
Love swells like the Solway, but ebbs like its tide —
And now am I come, with this lost love of mine,
To lead but one measure, drink one cup of wine.
There are maidens in Scotland more lovely by far,
That would gladly be bride to the young Lochinvar.'

The bride kiss'd the goblet: the knight took it up,
He quaff'd off the wine, and he threw down the cup.
She look'd down to blush, and she look'd up to sigh,
With a smile on her lips, and a tear in her eye.
He took her soft hand, ere her mother could bar, —
'Now tread we a measure!' said young Lochinvar.

So stately his form, and so lovely her face,
That never a hall such a galliard did grace;
While her mother did fret, and her father did fume,
And the bridegroom stood dangling his bonnet and plume;
And the bride-maidens whisper'd, ''Twere better by far,
To have match'd our fair cousin with young Lochinvar.'

One touch to her hand, and one word in her ear,
When they reach'd the hall-door, and the charger stood near;
So light to the croupe the fair lady he swung,
So light to the saddle before her he sprung!
'She is won! we are gone, over bank, bush, and scaur;
They'll have fleet steeds that follow,' quoth young Lochinvar.

There was mounting 'mong Græmes of the Netherby clan;
Forsters, Fenwicks, and Musgraves, they rode and they ran:
They was racing and chasing on Cannobie Lee,
But the lost bride of Netherby ne'er did they see.
So daring in love, and so dauntless in war,
Have ye e'er heard of gallant like young Lochinvar?

Sir Walter Scott

When I Roved a Young Highlander

When I roved a young Highlander o'er the dark heath,
   And climb'd thy steep summit, oh Morven of snow!
To gaze on the torrent that thunder'd beneath,
   Or the mist of the tempest that gather'd below.
Untutor'd by science, a stranger to fear,
   And rude as the rocks where my infancy grew,
No feeling, save one, to my bosom was dear;
   Need I say, my sweet Mary, 'twas centred in you?

Yet it could not be love, for I knew not the name, –
   What passion can dwell in the heart of a child?
But still I perceive an emotion the same
   As I felt, when a boy, on the crag-cover'd wild:
One image alone on my bosom impress'd,
   I loved my bleak regions, nor panted for new;
And few were my wants, for my wishes were bless'd;
   And pure were my thoughts, for my soul was with you.

I arose with the dawn; with my dog as my guide,
   From mountain to mountain I bounded along;
I breasted the billows of Dee's rushing tide,
   And heard at a distance the Highlander's song:
At eve, on my heath-cover'd couch of repose,
   No dreams, save of Mary, were spread to my view;
And warm to the skies my devotions arose,
   For the first of my prayers was a blessing on you.

I left my bleak home, and my visions are gone;
   The mountains are vanish'd, my youth is no more;
As the last of my race, I must wither alone,
   And delight but in days I have witness'd before:
Ah! splendour has raised but embitter'd my lot;
   More dear were the scenes which my infancy knew:
Though my hopes may have fail'd, yet they are not forgot;
   Though cold is my heart, still it lingers with you.

When I see some dark hill point its crest to the sky,
   I think of the rocks that o'ershadow Colbleen;
When I see the soft blue of a love-speaking eye,
   I think of those eyes that endear'd the rude scene;
When, haply, some light-waving locks I behold,
   That faintly resemble my Mary's in hue,
I think on the long, flowing ringlets of gold,
   The locks that were sacred to beauty, and you.

Yet the day may arrive when the mountains once more
   Shall rise to my sight in their mantles of snow:
But while these soar above me, unchanged as before,
   Will Mary be there to receive me? — ah, no!
Adieu, then, ye hills, where my childhood was bred!
   Though sweet flowing Dee, to thy waters adieu!
No home in the forest shall shelter my head, —
Ah! Mary, what home could be mine but with you?

George Gordon, Lord Byron

Tribute

glasgow's full of artists
they're three feet high
and eat sherbet dabs

Alan Jackson

The Good Thief

heh jimmy
yawright ih
stull wayz urryi
ih

heh jimmy
ma right insane yirra pape
ma right insane yirwanny uz jimmy

see it nyir eyes
wanny uz

heh

heh jimmy
lookslik wirgonny miss thi gemm
gonny miss thi GEMM jimmy
nearly three a cloke thinoo

dork init
good jobe theyve gote thi lights

Tom Leonard

The Great Ones

Ae morn aside the road frae Bray
  I wrocht my squad to mend the track;
A feck o' sodgers passed that way
  And garred me often straucht my back.

By cam a General on a horse,
  A jinglin' lad on either side.
I gie'd my best salute of course,
  Weel pleased to see sic honest pride.

And syne twae Frenchmen in a cawr –
  Yon are the lads to speel the braes;
They speldered me inch-deep wi' glaur
  And verra near ran ower my taes.

And last the pipes, and at their tail
  Oor gaucy lads in martial line.
I stopped my wark and cried them hail,
  And wished them weel for auld lang syne.

      . . .

An auld chap plooin' on the muir
  Ne'er jee'd his heid nor held his han',
But drave his furrow straucht and fair, –
  Thinks I, 'But ye're the biggest man.'

John Buchan

The Massacre of the Macpherson
[from the Gaelic]

Fhairshon swore a feud
  Against the clan M'Tavish;
Marched into their land
  To murder and to rafish;
For he did resolve
  To extirpate the vipers,
With four-and-twenty men
  And five-and-thirty pipers.

But when he had gone
  Half-way down Strath Canaan,
Of his fighting tail
  Just three were remainin'.
They were all he had,
  To back him in ta battle;
All the rest had gone
  Off, to drive ta cattle.

'Fery coot!' cried Fhairshon,
  'So my clan disgraced is;
Lads, we'll need to fight,
  Pefore we touch the peasties.
Here's Mhic-Mac-Methusaleh
  Coming wi' his tassals,
Gillies seventy-three,
  And sixty Dhuinéwassails!'

'Coot tay to you, sir;
  Are you not ta Fhairshon?
Was you coming here
  To fisit any person?
You are a plackguard, sir!
  It is now six hundred
Coot long years, and more,
  Since my glen was plundered.'

'Fat is tat you say?
　　Dare you cock your peaver?
I will teach you, sir,
　　Fat is coot pehaviour!
You shall not exist
　　For another day more;
I will shoot you, sir,
　　Or stap you with my claymore!'

'I am fery glad,
　　To learn what you mention,
Since I can prevent
　　Any such intention.'
So Mhic-Mac-Methusaleh
　　Gave some warlike howls,
Trew his skhian-dhu,
　　An' stuck it in his powels.

In this fery way
　　Tied ta faliant Fhairshon,
Who was always thought
　　A superior person.
Fhairshon had a son,
　　Who married Noah's daughter,
And nearly spoiled ta Flood,
　　By trinking up ta water:

Which he would have done,
　　I at least pelieve it,
Had ta mixture peen
　　Only half Glenlivet.
This is all my tale:
　　Sirs, I hope 'tis new t'ye!
Here's your fery good healths,
　　And tamn ta whusky duty!

W. E. Aytoun

TA
CRATUR.
ARK. INC.

Sunny Day

Vary auld
he stauns in his gairden
wi the sun ahint him.

He's near translucent.

Can I see richt
through him?

He doesnae ken I'm there.

I concentrate on his richt
ear. It glows wi licht
shinin through
but nocht is seen

through it

till he turns to me
wi a smile

and a pull
at his ear.

Duncan Glen

TATTIES

Gethsemane

Somewhere among the roses of the sky
slowly filling with birds and bushes
a star took root.
The evening trembled like a lake.
A drummer announced the arrival of darkness.

For those who slept under the rock
the leaves of the desert were sweet as honey,
the sun – full of bees,
and sand between the toes a fabulous sea
where Scripture walked.

No moon fell into the freezing stream
as midnight stilled the prayer-wheel.
A cur barked at the silence
at the empty features of the hills
and the old gods dying.

No waves ran into the parched mouth
nor shed doves over the burning head,
but a landscape haloed with lions
stoned into the postures of grief
unveiled a statue to love,

and a beggar's eyes
moved pride and defeat to prayers
for each heart that beats its weaving shreds
into the canvas vineyard
of a shroud of heirs.

J. F. Hendry

Anns A' Phàirce Mhóir

Falach-fead aig a' ghealaich,
siubhal-sìdhe miosg nan sgó,
a' chlann a' ruith a chéile
miosg adagan's a' Phàirce Mhóir.

Oidhche 'n deireadh an fhoghair
'n uair bha an Taghadh nas ciaire
's mu'n robh an saoghal 'na sgrìoban
cruaidhe dìreach giara.

'S gun fhios aig gille no nighinn
cia mhiad adag bh' air an raon,
a h-uile h-adag fhathast, dìomhair
mu'n robh an t-achadh 'na chlàr maol.

Cha robh an Taghadh cho soillcir
is sinne anns a' Phàirce Mhóir.

Somhairle MacGill-Eain

In the Big Park

The moon plays hide-and-seek,
gliding among the clouds,
the children chasing one another
among the stooks in the Big Park.

A night in late autumn
when the Election was dimmer
and before the world was
hard straight sharp furrows.

When no boy or girl knew
how many stooks were on the plain,
every stook still mysterious,
before the field was a bare expanse.

The Election was not clear
to us in the Big Park.

Sorley MacLean

Kirk Bell

Dove, unfurled twixt ark and sun,
Give Sabbath tongue!

Folk wind-burdened, fold wind-blown.
Dang-dang, ding-dong.

Birds howk long worms from the lawn.
The bronze vibrates.

A family goes, one long black line.
It romps and reels, the steeple!

Old Tabby licks the kipper bone.
'Come pray, good people!'

Six fine hats down one small lane.
The high mouth brims, berates.

The organ preludes, a solemn pain.
The bell is a folded dove again.

George Mackay Brown

Waddir-Wise

Dey telt me ninety million miles
O weary gait, an never wilt,
Yon glisk o sunlycht gligly fled
Afore hits fraacht o gold wis spilt.

Dey telt me o da clok o wind
Dis birlin Aert aroond him rowes,
Ey hentin in, an sae hit shaests
Fae crystal humps ta cloody howes.

Bit nane cood tell at wind an sun,
Baid blannabloora wi dy hair,
Wid spin a gilt an siller net
My een an illiss hert ta snare.

William J. Tait

November

Wailing-drunk
on a vicious wind
branches of oak
stagger and throw
handfuls of leaves
into the air.

Walter Perrie

105

Why the Poet Makes Poems

*(written to explain why I failed to keep an appointment
with my dentist, Dr K. P. Durkaez)*

When it's all done and said,
whether he is smithing away by the mad sea,
or, according to repute, silvering them in a garret
by moonlight, or in plush with a gold nib,
or plain bourgeois in a safe bungalow with a mortgage,
or in a place with a name, Paris, Warsaw, Edinburgh,
or sitting with his heart in the Highlands,
or taking time off at the office to pen a few words,
the whole business is a hang-over from the men in the trees,
when thunder and sun and quake and peas in a pod
were magic, and still is according to *his* book, admitting
botany is O.K. for the exposition of how the buds got there,
geology for how the rocks got just like that,
zoology for the how of the animals,
biology for us kind – but that's not his game:
  he's after the lion playing around with the lamb for fun.
He doesn't want to know the why. It's enough for him to say:
  'That's what's going on. The grass is jumping for joy,
and all the little fishes are laughing their heads off.'

George Bruce

Silva

The forest suffers material change, but yields
A lot that grows. The knowing firs that weep
Already; barb-head aspens; poplars blown
To silver half-tones; forest deeps at dawn
Of spruce, falling to make the evening times;
And subtler bocages and underwoods: they all
Go.
   Catalogues persist, and books
On epic catalogues, and diagrams of trees.

Alastair Fowler

Disbuddin

My faither is singin
a tune to himsel
in his gairden.

He's disbuddin
chrysanthemums
to create large
single blooms
he kens he'll ne'er see.

He's near tone deif
but likes hymn tunes
rendered wi gusto.

He disnae believe
in God

and has nae answers

but to accept
the disbuddin

wi a sang ...

Duncan Glen

After the Market

The pens are empty now, the ring is quiet;
the shepherds spit and laugh, and lean on crooks;
the bargains made with drams to wet the diet
are good or bad, but writ in hands, not books.

A fat young country woman with big feet,
a child on arm, another at the knee,
bullies a reeling drover down the street,
dividing her care fairly between three.

The bidding's stopped and slap of palm on palm
is sealed forever; all is dealt and done.
They stand awhile under the twilit calm,
then shrug their collars up and head for home.

William Neill

All the Families

Everything clusters. Willows and sallows
Flock to the bottoms, feeling for water,
Finding it where the myrtles gather
And cows, knee-deep in the lochan,
Twitch at the hordes of the midges.
Blood-drops bunch on the rowans
Which neighbour the ends of the houses.

The village huddles beside the sea-loch,
Sheltering under a scree of boulders
Where a squadron of Norsemen landed
And swarmed again to seaward,
Following shoals of herring and mackerel.
Brown sails thronged to the fishing,
The families crowded the shingle,
Splitting and salting, cramming the barrels.

In the War they died in battalions.

In the glade of the birches and firs
The graves of the village are single
As survivors marooned on an island,
Too stunned to speak to each other.
Coveys of grouse cowered in the heather
While grey sheep strayed and foraged
Like lice in the seams of the moorland.
In the car-park tourists jostled
And went south like the wheatears in autumn.

Now salmon seethe in the fish-farm.
The new white houses nestle
And cows crowd to the gate at gloaming.
Even in winter the windows are beacons
And the foreshore hotches with children.

David Craig

109

Snapshot

Swaddled nine months old
in warm winter woollens
('He mustn't catch cold')
fat as a policeman,
I am held head-high
by proud grandfather.

Behind thin gold
spectacles his blue eyes
smile relief at this bold
progeny, the first-come,
ensuring the family,
and laughing fit to burst.

Now, to wonder at, I hold
the photograph and the moment,
cherishing that fond old
man, the laughing child
so confident in love and fuss.

Whatever happened to the two of us?

Ken Morrice

Late Autumn

Though leaves of glass fall whole

                     where they may lie,

there are still flowers about
under a flamingo sky
and spring will come again

                     bringing crocus and the rose,

if not for those
who live for time and history,
like flies in amber,
building walls of frozen glory

                     to keep their winter in.

J. F. Hendry

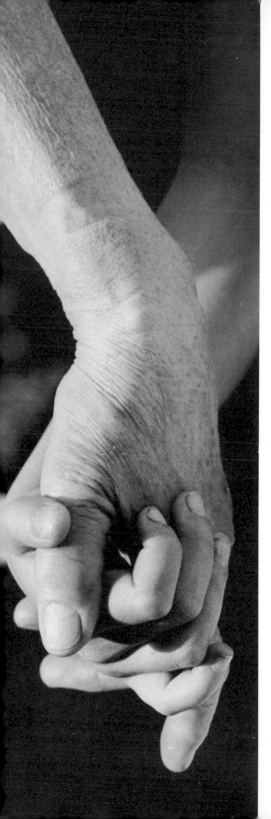

Savings

She saved her money
And she hid her money in
An oriental tin
That came from Twining's Tea.
– 'Oh, how much money have you now?'
But she'd never let me see.
She'd place that tin into my hands,
Then with her hands on mine
She'd help me shake her Twining's tin –
Half-crowns and a sovereign,
Shillings, sixpences and florins
Rattled on the paper notes.
That was her funeral fund
I was too young to understand.
When I did, and she was dead,
It wasn't death that I could see
In tea-leaves sifting from a spoon
That came out of a Chinese tin.
I saw the life she'd shovelled in.

Douglas Dunn

111

The Green Gate

So Mansie came to the green gate.
A hooded man
Asked Mansie what he wanted.
Mansie said, 'Nothing. I came here
Because the road
Stops here (it seems) and I always have a word
At an open door, going past.
I have nothing in my hand. I'm sorry.
Seventy years with plough and boat
And never a gift!'
The grave voice said, 'Not an illustrious life.
But come in, traveller.
Such as it is, you have a story to tell
Different from the memoirs of clown and king,
And here
Simplicity is something.'
Mansie went in, clothed with his days
And sat down
At a table with six quiet strangers.
There was food and drink on the board,
From hand to hand a weaving of good courtesy
On a loom of silence.
Then a child said to Mansie
'The face of the man at the gate,
I saw it,
And it was brighter than the sun.'
Their tongues were unlocked at the table then.
Far into the night
They told, one after other, their stories:
Pure as root or shell or star.
Listening, Mansie considered
His days of clay and sweat and dung
And he shook his head.
But when he stood by the fire at last
His mouth was a harp. His mouth was a struck harp.

George Mackay Brown

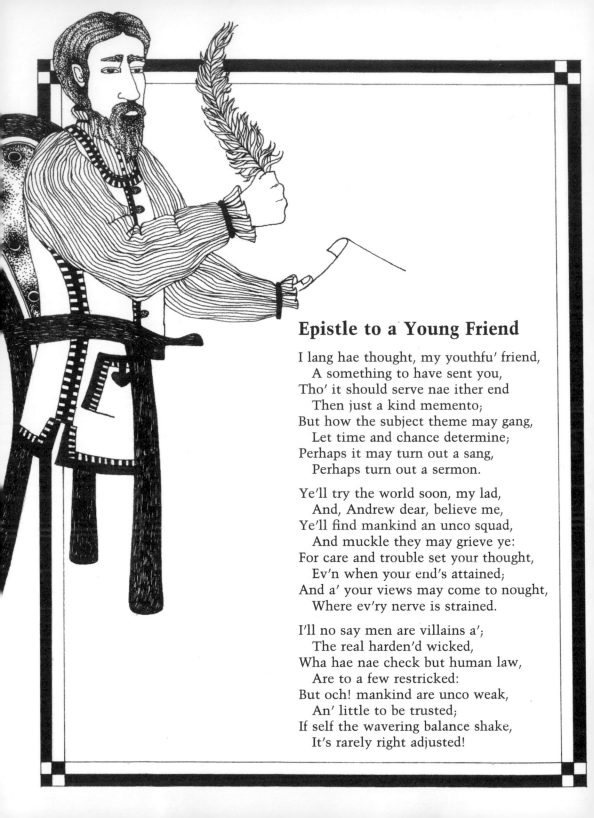

Epistle to a Young Friend

I lang hae thought, my youthfu' friend,
  A something to have sent you,
Tho' it should serve nae ither end
  Then just a kind memento;
But how the subject theme may gang,
  Let time and chance determine;
Perhaps it may turn out a sang,
  Perhaps turn out a sermon.

Ye'll try the world soon, my lad,
  And, Andrew dear, believe me,
Ye'll find mankind an unco squad,
  And muckle they may grieve ye:
For care and trouble set your thought,
  Ev'n when your end's attained;
And a' your views may come to nought,
  Where ev'ry nerve is strained.

I'll no say men are villains a';
  The real harden'd wicked,
Wha hae nae check but human law,
  Are to a few restricked:
But och! mankind are unco weak,
  An' little to be trusted;
If self the wavering balance shake,
  It's rarely right adjusted!

Yet they wha fa' in fortune's strife,
  Their fate we shouldna censure;
For still th' important end of life
  They equally may answer.
A man may hae an honest heart,
  Tho' poortith hourly stare him;
A man may tak a neibor's part,
  Yet hae nae cash to spare him.

Aye free, aff han', your story tell,
  When wi' a bosom crony;
But still keep something to yoursel
  Ye scarcely tell to ony.
Conceal yoursel as weel's ye can
  Frae critical dissection;
But keek thro' ev'ry other man
  Wi' sharpen'd sly inspection.

The sacred lowe o' weel-plac'd love,
  Luxuriantly indulge it;
But never tempt th' illicit rove,
  Tho' naething should divulge it:
I wave the quantum o' the sin,
  The hazard of concealing;
But och! it hardens a' within,
  And petrifies the feeling!

To catch dame Fortune's golden smile,
  Assiduous wait upon her;
And gather gear by ev'ry wile
  That's justified by honour;
Not for to hide it in a hedge,
  Nor for a train attendant;
But for the glorious privilege
  Of being independent.

The fear o' hell's a hangman's whip
  To haud the wretch in order;
But where ye feel your honour grip,
  Let that aye be your border:
Its slightest touches, instant pause
  Debar a' side pretences;
And resolutely keep its laws,
  Uncaring consequences.

The great Creator to revere
    Must sure become the creature;
But still the preaching cant forbear,
    And ev'n the rigid feature:
Yet ne'er with wits profane to range
    Be complaisance extended;
An atheist laugh 's a poor exchange
    For Deity offended.

When ranting round in pleasure's ring,
    Religion may be blinded;
Or, if she gie a random sting,
    It may be little minded;
But when on life we're tempest-driv'n,
    A conscience but a canker –
A correspondence fix'd wi' Heav'n
    Is sure a noble anchor.

Adieu, dear amiable youth!
    Your heart can ne'er be wanting!
May prudence, fortitude, and truth
    Erect your brow undaunting.
In ploughman phrase, God send you speed
    Still daily to grow wiser;
And may ye better reck the rede
Than ever did th' adviser!

Robert Burns

A Country Tale

Hugh, beachcomber
Fell so much in love with Anna, farmer's daughter,
He promised her everything,
All the wealth of the sea,
Coral, pearl, broken sea-chests.

And Anna stood at last in the barn with Hugh
In front of the minister,
Book and ring between them,
Hugh in a lobster-blue suit, Anna
White and flowing as milk.

Next morning, after the wedding feast
Hugh took the bride over the hill
Down to the shore.
And he led her through the door of his bothy.
It didn't look
Like the castle of a sea prince.
Inside
Were two hard chairs, a hard bed, a board,
A candle stump in a bottle.
The cupboard had only
A bowl of whelks, and a bottle of rum
Flung up by the waves.

Anna said nothing. She thought
'Tomorrow he'll show me
The chest of pearls, for sure.'
Hugh, whelk-full, rum-ruddy
Said, 'Bed-time. I must
Be up early. A good wind for sea-wrack, this,
A six-day heave from the west.'
His snores
Made the shanty shake. Anna
Put driftwood on the fire.
She sat beside the little flame. She had soon,
Two tears, like pearls, on her face.

Every sunset
Hugh came up from the beach, burdened.
Driftwood aslope on his shoulder.
A melon round as the moon
But bitter as Gomorrah.
A crab or two with clashing armoured thumbs.
A boot, gaping,
He swore could be mended with a dozen nails.
Whelks, a small lobster,
A sweetness of dulse, and once
A jointed whale's backbone.

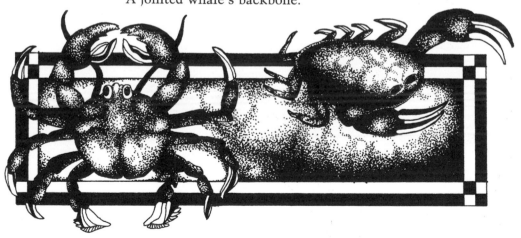

(In winter
Most days, it was too stormy
To venture along the beach.
But afterwards, in the silence, tawdry troves.)

One night when the rain
Made songs on the little dark window candle-splashed,
Said Anna
'Where's the pearl, man? Where
Are the torrents of sea silver?'

Hugh listened to the harps of rain.
He said, 'I hope, lass,
A wave throws up a case of aquavit
From the Norsky wreck,
Or it's a poor Yule for you and me.
(One bottle of gin would do.)'

Anna's face was a washed stone.
She dreamed often
Of peatfires, cornstalks, cows,
Round cheeses, yellow cubes of butter,
The horse in a spring wind, whirling a sun hoof.

She whispered in March
Upon the crib and the sea-cold baby,
'Buddo, your dad
Is down at the shore. He's seeking
The one pearl
That will make us unpoor and prosperous.
The sea-girls are jealous (he says).
They will not give him the treasure.
He has married a corn and butter lass.
The sea-girls give him only
Small bitter kisses. He'll soon be home,
That liar,
His face all love and coldness and loss.
But you, my pet, I'll take you
Over the hill to the farm,
To the barking dog and the fiddle,
To horsemen ruddy with ale,
To the glebe gold
Grained, since harvest, through earth-dark fingers' ...

Then Hugh came in,
An ivory harp on his shoulder.

George Mackay Brown

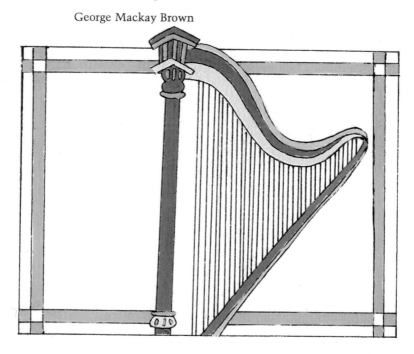

'The vales, the vocal hills'
[from *Lochleven*]

The vales, the vocal hills,
The woods, the waters, and the heart of man
Send out a gen'ral song; 'tis beauty all
To poet's eye and music to his ear.

Michael Bruce

Archives

generation upon
generation upon
generation upon
generation upon
generation upon
generation upon
generation upon
generation upon
generation upon
generation upon
generation upon
generation upon
generation upon
generation upon
generation upon
generation upon
generation upon
generation upon
generation upon
g neration upon
g neration up n
g nerat on up n
g nerat   n p n
g nerat   n p n
g   erat   n p n
g   era   n p n
g   era   n   n
g   er   n   n
g   r   n   n
g   n   n
g   n
g

Edwin Morgan

Glossary of Scots Words

Freedom
maiss: makes
liking: liberty
na ellis nocht: nor
    anything else
gif: if
dome: doom
thyrldome: slavery
perquer: by heart

Winter-Time
lowe: light, glow
fit: foot
ghaisty: ghostly
howe: hollow
sheda: shadow
howlet: owl, owlet
can'els: candles
shoon: shoes
soughin': sighing
freit: superstitious fancy

Sea Ballad
waukrife: wakeful
her lane: by herself
weidie: widow
wydan: wading
leesome lane: quite alone
selkies: seals
santit: vanished

The Years of the Crocodile
solsequium: the Zodiac
secutit: followed
lum hat: 'chimney-pot' hat
grat: wept

Hungry Waters
daberlack: leek-like
    lengths of seaweed
dackered: searched

The Talk of the Headlands
rienge: range

The Bubblyjock
bubblyjock: turkey
bogle: scarecrow
bouks: hiccups
raxin: stretching
chouks: jaws
syne: then
blether: bladder

Hal o' The Wynd
wynd: narrow lane
skinklin: glittering
douce: gentle
draik: drench
drouth: thirst
clappering: rattling
speer: ask questions
dawties: darlings
dirlin: thrilling

Brigs o' Braid
haugh: river-meadow
slae: sloe
houlets: owls
freshets: freshwater streams
buss: bush
fremit: strange
wight: fellow
riped: searched
pooch: pocket
stown: stolen
chappit: struck
scour: search
howff: tavern
pen: alleyway
dawin: dawn
dowf: sad
steeks: stitches

Crowdieknowe
loupin: jumping
feck: great deal
fegs: faith
blate: cautious
gin: if

Lochinvar
scaur: crag

The Flowers of the Forest
yowe: ewe
loaning: meadow
buchts: sheep folds
dowie: dull
wae: woeful
daffin': jesting
gabbin': chattering
leglen: milk-pail
hairst: harvest
lyart: grizzled
runkled: wrinkled
fleeching: beseeching
swankies: lusty lads
bogle: hide and seek

The Great Ones
feck: great deal
garred: made
cawr: car
speel: climb
speldered: spattered
glaur: mud
gaucy: jolly

Waddir-Wise
dey: they
waddir: weather
gait: motion
wilt: strayed
glisk: gleam
gligly: quickly
hits: its

fraacht: burden
da: the
aert: earth
rowes: wraps
hentin: gathering
shaests: chases
baid: both
blannabloora: in
     conspiracy (with)
illiss: unsuspecting

Epistle to a Young Friend
unco: strange, mighty
muckle: much
poortith: poverty
cronie: friend
keek: look
lowe: flame
tempt: attempt
ranting: frolicking
reck the rede: heed the
     counsel

Index of First Lines

Ae morn aside the road frae Bray 98
A flop 68
A! fredome is a noble thing! 12
Am I either? 34
A myriad tides have foamed 55
And she came home 14
An unborn bird lies crumpled and curled 7
As slowly as the moon he woke 64
At twelve years old I drove a sweating pair 57
A waukrife weidie on the sand 42

Barely a twelvemonth after 72
Beneath the horror of a rock 61
Between two mighty hills a sheer 63
Bha 'n ulaidh an leth-fhalach 18
Break – break it open; let the knocker rust 6
Breathes there the man, with soul so dead 9

Comin hame fae school aince I met 36

Dey telt me ninety million miles 105
Dove, unfurled twixt ark and sun 104
Drifting too near the Roznian coast 50

Everything clusters. Willows and sallows 109

Falach-fead aig a' ghealaich 103
Fhairshon swore a feud 99

generation upon 122
glasgow's full of artists 96
great 60

Hal o' the Wynd he taen the field 75
Hame, hame, hame, hame fain wad I be 13
heh jimmy 97
He snuffles towards 71
Hugh, beachcomber 117

I called her fig, I called her pog 69
I could tell 24
I held the lead pencil 66
I lang hae thought, my youthfu' friend 114
I leave my body in a new blue suit 25
I marched along the cliff 49
In orange sweater, and blue, bulging jeans 81
In their 31

In the years o the maytree 46
I saw a live whale once 48
It's half like a bird and half like a bogle 62
I've heard the lilting at our yowe-milking 91

Land of great heathered hills 10
Last night a wind from Lammermoor came roaring up the glen 74
Lowpers, gowpers 17

Millions and millions of stars 33
Monday, at the gloamin' 29
My chum Eric was well-behaved 38
My faither is singin 107

Now the earth has stopped rising 83

October winds are over the Lammermuirs 76
'O, Davie Loch, get up and gae 78
Oh to be at Crowdieknowe 90
O, young Lochinvar is come out of the west 92

plane crossing 22
pléin a dol tarsuing 22

Says Ebbing Point to Laggan Head 54
Scotland small? Our multiform, our infinite Scotland *small?* 8
She saved her money 111
She was the extra decoy 58
So Mansie came to the green gate 112
Some stuff about the moon 21
Sometimes at night when the wind blows hard 52
Sometimes when I watch TV 15
Somewhere among the roses of the sky 102
Swaddled nine months old 110

The auld men o' the sea 45
The forest suffers material change, but yields 107
The moon plays hide-and-seek 103
The pens are empty now, the ring is quiet 108
The pond has closed its frozen eyelid 80
There's a hill in the Lomonds 23
There were twa brethren in the north 88
The treasure was half-hidden 18
The trunks of great Brazilian balsa trees 84
The vales; the vocal hills 121
Though leaves of glass fall whole 110

Vary auld 101

Wailing drunk 105
water 53

Waterwheels in 56
wave 44
We are all in the stars 19
We who live by the eye 16
When I leave school I want to be 39
When I no more behold thee 86
When I roved a young Highlander o'er the dark heath 94
When it's all done and said 106
Who was I to deny a headstrong balloon 26

You, little rugged boy without seat to your trousers 40

Acknowledgements

The Editor and Publisher wish to thank the following for permission to reprint copyright poems in this anthology.

Marion Angus: 'Winter-Time' from *The Singin' Lass*. Reprinted by permission of Faber & Faber Ltd. Robin Bell: 'The Wooden Curlew'; 'The Owl', © 1985 Robin Bell. John Bett: 'You're Late Again Kathleen', © 1985 John Bett. David Black: 'The Educators' (Barrie and Rockcliff/The Cresset Press, 1969). By permission of the author. Alan Bold: 'The Gliders', © 1985 Alan Bold. George Mackay Brown: 'A Country Tale'; 'The Green Gate'; 'Kirk Bell', © 1985 George Mackay Brown. George Bruce: 'Why the Poet Makes Poems', © 1985 George Bruce. John Buchan: 'The Great Ones'. Reprinted by permission of The Right Honourable Lord Tweedsmuir CBE and A.P. Watt Ltd. Tom Buchan: 'Submarine' © 1969, Tom Buchan from *Dolphins at Cochin* (Barrie & Rockliff, 1969); 'The Loch Ness Monster' c 1972, Tom Buchan, from *Poems 1969–72*. Reprinted by permission of the author. David Craig: 'All the Families', © 1985 David Craig. Douglas Dunn: 'Lost Gloves' from *Barbarians*; 'Savings' from *St. Kilda's Parliament*. Reprinted by permission of Faber & Faber Ltd. Ian Hamilton Finlay: 'Wave/Rock', 'The Boat's Blue Print', 'water wheels in whirl' and 'Great Frog Race' in *Poems To Hear and See* (Macmillan: New York, 1971). Reprinted by permission of the author. Alastair Fowler: 'Silva', 'Pignsypogsny', © 1985 Alastair Fowler. Duncan Glen: 'Disbuddin'; 'Sunny Day', 1985 © Duncan Glen. Andrew Greig: 'War-Dream', © 1985 Andrew Greig. George Campbell Hay: 'The Talk of the Headlands' from *Wind on Loch Fyne* (1948). Reprinted by permission of the author. J.F. Hendry: 'Gethsemane'; 'Late Autumn', © 1985 J.F. Hendry. Alan Jackson: 'This Nor That' (previously unpublished) © 1985 Alan Jackson; 'Tribute' and 'great' from *The Grim Wayfarer* (Fulcrum). Reprinted by permission of the author. Kathleen Jamie: 'The philosopher stops work to look out of the window', © 1985 Kathleen Jamie. William Jeffrey: 'Seaweed'. Reprinted by permission of Mrs. Margaret W.J. Jeffrey. Tom Leonard: 'The Good Thief' from *Intimate Voices: 1965–83* (Galloping Dog Press, Newcastle). Reprinted by permission of the author. Maurice Lindsay: 'The Clown', © 1985 Maurice Lindsay. George MacBeth: 'The Guy' © George Macbeth 1983. Norman MacCaig: 'Blind Horse'; 'Whales'; 'End of a cold night', © 1985 Norman MacCaig. Hugh MacDiarmid: 'The Bubblyjock'; 'Crowdieknowe'; 'Scotland small?' and 'Hungry Waters'. Reprinted by permission of the Executor of the Hugh MacDiarmid Estate. Forbes MacGregor: 'Brigs o'Braid', © 1985 Forbes MacGregor. A.D. Mackie: 'Sea Ballad', © 1985 A.D. Mackie. Alastair Mackie: 'At tea-time', © 1985 Alastair Mackie. Sorley MacLean: 'Anns a' Phàirce Mhóir/In The Big Park' from *Springtide and Neaptide* (Canongate). Reprinted by permission of the author. Aonghas MacNeacail: 'gleann fadamach/glen remote', © 1985 Aonghas MacNeacail. William Montgomerie: 'UFO', © 1985 William Montgomerie. Edwin Morgan: 'Archives' from *Poems of Thirty Years* (Carcanet Press, 1982). Reprinted by permission of the author. Ken Morrice: 'Little by little' and 'Snapshot', © 1985 Ken Morrice.

Edwin Muir: 'The Horses' from *The Collected Poems of Edwin Muir*. Reprinted by permission of Faber & Faber Ltd. William Soutar: 'Hal O'The Wynd'; 'Local Habitation'. Reprinted by the Trustees of the National Library of Scotland. William Neill: 'Cart Wheels' and 'After the Market', © 1985 William Neill. Walter Perrie: 'Proverb' and 'November', © 1985 Walter Perrie. Tessa Ransford: 'Television People' © 1985 Tessa Ransford. Alexander Scott: 'Top of the Pops' from *Selected Poems 1943–1974* (Akros, 1975). Reprinted by permission of the author, Francis George Scott: Scottish National Anthem. For permission to print music by acknowledgement is made to George Scott. Tom Scott: 'Hopes', © 1985 Tom Scott. Iain Crichton Smith: 'TV'; 'A Summary of *A Midsummer Night's Dream*'; 'When I Leave School'; 'At School', © 1985 Iain Crichton Smith. Sydney Goodsir Smith: 'The Year of the Crocodile' from *Collected Poems* by Sydney Goodsir Smith, published by John Calder (Publishers) Ltd., is reproduced by kind permission of the publishers. William J. Tait: 'Waddir-wise'. First appeared in *New Shetlander* 1949/50. Reprinted by permission of the author. Ruaraidh MacThomais/Derick Thomson: 'Ulaidh/Treasure', © 1985 Ruaraidh MacThomais/Derick Thomson. Sydney Tremayne: 'Small Boy and Lighthouse'. Reprinted by permission of the author. John Whitworth: 'Precisely to Scale', © 1985 John Whitworth.

Illustrated by: Ann McCormack, Bob Dewar, Julie Lacome, Alyson MacNeill, Iain Piercy.